EXCEL STUDIES IN LITERATURE

General Editor: Dr Barry Spurr

THE POETRY
OF
EMILY DICKINSON

Barry Spurr

with an introduction on 'Reading Poetry'

PASCAL
PRESS

Dr Barry Spurr MA MLitt PhD MACE is Senior Lecturer in English Literature at the University of Sydney and Inaugural University of Sydney Fellow in English at Sydney Grammar School.

© Barry Spurr 1994

ISBN 1 875777 25 3

Pascal Press
PO Box 250
Glebe NSW 2037

Printed in Australia by Australian Print Group.

THE POETRY OF EMILY DICKINSON

CONTENTS

GENERAL EDITOR'S INTRODUCTION

The purpose of every study in this series is to provide a thorough, helpful and stimulating account of the author and text under consideration.

In the past, such guides have either unsatisfactorily reduced, to summary and point form, the complexities of literary texts, or have provided extended commentaries that have been inappropriate both for students' needs in preparation for essays and examinations, and for teachers' requirements in the classroom.

The titles in the **Excel Studies in Literature** series cover a wide range of texts in poetry, drama and the novel, and include several studies of the works of significant Australian authors which have not received detailed treatment before. The contributing authors to the series are all convinced of the necessity to provide students with structured literary analyses that are of the highest quality, while being lucid and comprehensible and immediately relevant to essay and examination preparation. Above all, they seek to convey a sense of the enjoyment which comes from the careful and imaginative reading of books.

The purpose of this series will have been fulfilled if the students and teachers who use these studies find them to be useful and encouraging in their reading and understanding of literature.

Dr Barry Spurr
Department of English,
University of Sydney.

READING POETRY

Poetry is written neither to be analysed nor to be the subject of examination questions. It is written to be enjoyed.

Poets want their work to captivate us, by showing us new ways of seeing commonplace events or experiences, or by introducing us to extraordinary aspects of life. To achieve this, poets use a variety of strategies of communication and techniques of language. Poetry is as remarkable for the host of ways in which poets have chosen to write — their 'style' — as for their numerous subjects or themes.

Poetry may entertain or amuse us, simply by its humorous content. Or the writer may use comedy to make a more serious point. This is usually the method of satirical poets. Again, a poem might move us to tears, or challenge (or confirm) our convictions about politics, morality or religion. Poetry can excite us, sadden us or terrify us. In one way or another, a good poem usually disturbs our equilibrium, or stability, pricking our conscience, lifting our heart or engaging our mind. Poets encourage us to explore and celebrate our humanity in all its diversity: its joy, its tragedy, its mystery.

For this reason, a poem should never be narrowly approached as a puzzle to be solved, or an exercise to be studied. Poetry *is* often puzzling and, as every school student knows, poems *are* set for study. But to appreciate poetry — and, so, to make its difficulties easier to approach and its study less laborious — it is vital to come to it with expectations appropriate to the richest form of literary expression known to humanity.

The reason why poems are often complex in style and concentrated in meaning is that they embody intensities of thought and emotion. Moreover, because poetry is the most compressed of literary forms, these elements are further intensified by the poet's use of technical conventions — as in the fourteen-line sonnet, or a lyric's four-line stanzas. It is through these intensifications of matter and method that poets are able to strike to the heart of human experience, in language, and we should not be discouraged if a poem does not reveal its full meaning immediately. On the contrary, it would be a disappointingly shallow work if it did. The greatest poems repay numerous re-readings throughout our lives. We can return to them, time and again, and find different nuances and new delight in the writer's accomplishment. The same is true, of course, of great music and of the great masterpieces of painting. They are inexhaustible. But the direct result of that truth is the recognition that artistry and expression that endure, unlike ephemeral productions, are unlikely to satisfy our desires for instant gratification. The appreciation of poetry requires patience, application, intelligence and sensitivity — like anything that is worthwhile in life.

> **The reason why poems are often complex in style and concentrated in meaning is that they embody intensities of thought and emotion.**

In our reading of poetry, several steps should be taken as we come to know a poem and enjoy it.

READING ALOUD

The first stage in the appreciation of a poem, after we have cast our eyes over it silently to gain an idea of its organisation and character, is to read it out loud — whether we are alone or in class.

Poets want their words, images, rhymes and rhythms to be heard and savoured, just as composers intend their musical notation to be brought to life in performance. By reading aloud — a slower process than reading silently — we are encouraged to concentrate more carefully on the words. Also we discover then, and in subsequent re-readings, how the aural qualities of the language of a good poem can be as important to its message as the meaning of the vocabulary the poet has used.

Sweet-sounding words and a gentle, song-like rhythm amplify the tender emotion of love which a poet might want to convey:

> Drink to me only with thine eyes,
> And I will pledge with mine;
> Or leave a kiss but in the cup,
> And I'll not look for wine.

Ben Jonson: 'To Celia'

Harsh words and a pointed rhythm convey a very different emotion:

> Break, break, break,
> On thy cold grey stones, O Sea!

Alfred, Lord Tennyson: 'Break, Break, Break'

An elevated language and imagery give us the sense of celebration, in resonant polysyllabic words:

> Where the bright Seraphim in burning row
> Their loud up-lifted Angel trumpets blow
> And the Cherubic host in thousand quires
> Touch their immortal Harps of golden wires.

John Milton: 'At a Solemn Music'

Then, in T.S Eliot's *The Waste Land*, the sense of despair and desolation in life is unforgettably enunciated in the haunting monotony of poetry that conveys the condition of contemporary existence (as many twentieth-century poets have interpreted it):

> Under the brown fog of a winter dawn,
> A crowd flowed over London Bridge, so many,
> I had not thought death had undone so many.
> Sighs, short and infrequent, were exhaled,
> And each man fixed his eyes before his feet.

In each of these examples (the number of which could be multiplied endlessly) we find that by *hearing* what the poet is saying, as we read him, our understanding is enriched.

Careful reading aloud, moreover, in alerting us to the rhythmic pulse of verse, assists our appreciation of meaning, for a skilful poet will make the emphases fall on key words:

> Remember me when I am gone away,
> Gone far away into the silent land.

Christina Rossetti: 'Remember'

Here, 'gone' and 'away' forcefully stress the future absence of the speaker and the finality of her departure. Rhythm and repetition are often found together in poetry.

Reading aloud, finally, is an aid to memory. If you become accustomed to *speaking* poetry, you will memorise it. This is helpful in examinations, but — far more importantly — a memorised poem will become part of you, for life. Such memorising is unfashionable today, but it is an invaluable aid to the appreciation of literature. No one who has ever committed the following lines, for example, to memory could ever forget them:

> Tyger! Tyger! burning bright
> In the forests of the night,
> What immortal hand or eye
> Could frame thy fearful symmetry?

> **William Blake**: 'The Tyger'

Memorising is unfashionable today, but it is an invaluable aid to the appreciation of literature.

And the same is true of poems that, although less obviously memorable because of a simple rhythm and rhyme, have a power of expression that abides in our minds:

> Death, be not proud, though some have called thee
> Mighty and dreadful, for thou art not so.

> **John Donne**: Holy Sonnet 10

Or a profundity of sentiment:

> Far from the madding crowd's ignoble strife,
> Their sober wishes never learned to stray;
> Along the cool sequestered vale of life
> They kept the noiseless tenor of their way.

> **Thomas Gray**: 'Elegy Written in a Country
> Churchyard'

Or their power to move through striking visual imagery:

> Nobody heard him, the dead man,
> But still he lay moaning:
> I was much further out than you thought
> And not waving but drowning.

Stevie Smith: 'Not Waving but Drowning'.

DESCRIBING A POEM

Having read a poem out loud and gauged something of its subject matter, its mood and its tone, and having checked the meanings of obscure words or references, we will want to deepen our appreciation of its artistry by a more formal and disciplined account of it, and in turn to communicate our enjoyment to others.

This is the justification of that often maligned discipline of literary criticism: to understand and appreciate works of literary art and to share that understanding and appreciation. Thus conceived, literary criticism is an invaluable aid to the reading of poetry. It is justly rebuked, however, when it becomes so obscure as to conceal the meaning of literature, rather than reveal it, or when under the guise of literary appreciation, it serves some ideological purpose of the critic, rather than seeking objectively to throw light upon the ideas of the author.

A sequence of steps in the description of a poem will assist our approach to it.

BIOGRAPHY

The first step in describing a poem is biographical. We need to identify its author, acknowledging that poetry, like all artistic expression, has its origin in the experience of its creator. It is not limited by that experience, for the poet in publishing the poem has made its theme and expression available to others for their interpretation. But it is futile to contend that the author's identity and biography are irrelevant to the understanding of the work he or she produced.

> **It is futile to contend that the author's identity and biography are irrelevant to the understanding of the work he or she produced.**

In Robert Lowell's *Life Studies*, for example, the emphasis is on the particular — even peculiar — biographies of Lowell and his family: the reader who is informed about the poet's biography will bring valuable understanding to the interpretation of many details in these poems. Yet *Life Studies* is also a larger statement about the character of Western (in particular American) civilisation in the later twentieth century. *Life Studies* is about Lowell's life and life in general.

For this reason when a poet speaks in the first person ('I') in a poem, it is possible that he intends either to reveal himself directly or to personalise a more general experience (such as being in love). It is best, therefore, when referring to the speaker in a poem to use precisely that term — 'speaker' — rather than to name the poet directly. In many poems, poets have used the first person fictionally to give an air of intimacy, but not necessarily to transcribe directly what they have

11

experienced in their own lives.

In other words, poems are, in varying degrees, autobiographical. Some, such as many of those of George Herbert and Philip Larkin, speak directly from their writer's experience:

> I struck the board and cried: 'No more;
> I will abroad!'

George Herbert : 'The Collar'

> That Whitsun, I was late getting away:
> Not till about
> One-twenty on the sunlit Saturday.

Philip Larkin:'The Whitsun Weddings'

But this does not mean that we cannot identify with the circumstances they recount.

Other writers are so universal as to conceal individual details:

> All human things are subject to decay,
> And when fate summons, monarchs must obey.

John Dryden:'Mac Flecknoe'

However, even in works of epic scope, such as Milton's *Paradise Lost*, or a philosophical poem like Eliot's *Four Quartet*s, the personality of the author reveals itself in subtle ways. The very strategy to attempt to universalise one's emotions and experience, of course, is itself a trait of an individual personality.

HISTORY

Our appreciation of the significance of a writer's biography, the history of a life, leads on to the next stage in the reading of a poem — some knowledge of the history of the period in which it was written. Having set the poem in the context of the author's biography, we need to see it in the larger setting of its times. It matters, to the reading of a poem, whether (for example) it was written in nineteenth-century England or twentieth-century Australia.

William Blake's poetry, for instance, vividly evokes his response to the world of the Industrial Revolution as he had observed it in London two hundred years ago. To read his *Songs of Innocence and Experience* without some knowledge of that momentous social phenomenon would severely limit our appreciation of his critique as presented in his poetry. Similarly, William Wordsworth's Romantic revulsion from the spirit of his time requires familiarity with that time if we are to take his response seriously:

> Milton! thou shouldst be living at this hour:
> England hath need of thee: she is a fen
> Of stagnant waters.
> 'London, 1802'

In reading Sylvia Plath's tortured account of her sufferings, in the *Ariel* collection published after her suicide in 1963, we might think it sufficient to have some details of her private life. But these works are also public documents. The progression of Plath's poetry from the 1950s to the 1960s reflects not only her private anguish but the tensions of Western society in those years.

13

The need to bring historical learning to the reading of poetry may seem daunting, but the most important requirement is simply to be on our guard against assuming that we may read poetry from different ages and cultures in the same way that we read poems by contemporary writers and friends, whose ideas are so close to our own. It is arrogant and ignorant to bring twentieth-century assumptions to the readings of works from previous ages and to suppose that our view of things is the only view and superior to those of men and women who have lived in the past.

> **It is arrogant and ignorant to bring twentieth-century assumptions to the readings of works from previous ages.**

Poetry anthologies, in which poems are gathered by theme, run the risk of obscuring the very real differences in interpretation of subjects which occur as we move from century to century, culture to culture. One I have seen has a section on 'Death' and puts together John Donne's famous sonnet on that subject (to which we have already referred) and Philip Larkin's poem, 'Days':

> Where can we live but days?
> Ah, solving that question
> Brings the priest and the doctor
> In their long coats
> Running over the fields.

The problem here is that the attitudes of Donne and Larkin to death are so unlike that they might be writing about different subjects. While Donne proclaimed the annihilation of death, Larkin was obsessed with its reality (and, for reasons which we

14

will consider in the next section, they address the issue in very dissimilar styles of poetry). The explanation of this difference is to be discovered in the profound spirituality of the seventeenth-century writer, which reflects the God-centred character of his age, and the sceptical agnosticism of the twentieth-century poet which speaks of his times.

The impact of poems is lessened if we are not alert to the different world-views from which they proceed. Part of the excitement (and humane value) of poetry is the window it provides into preoccupations and convictions at once so remote from our own, yet part of us, as we are part of human history.

A sense of the past, and a knowledge about it, are vital to the intelligent reading of poetry.

LITERARY HISTORY

In addition to a broad understanding of history as the background to the subjects and concerns of poets from different centuries, we also need more specialist knowledge of literary history, of the artistic movements to which poets belong. For these 'schools' are characterised by certain ideas about poetry - its matter and manner.

The greatest poets are usually innovators, initiating artistic movements to which a generation or more of writers subscribe. So John Donne, for example, began the so-called 'Metaphysical' school, in the early seventeenth century; John Dryden anticipated the Augustanism of the eighteenth century; Wordsworth and Coleridge were the initiators of Romanticism in the nineteenth century, and T.S. Eliot was the first of the Modernist poets a century later.

15

> **The greatest poets are usually innovators,
> initiating artistic movements to which a generation
> or more of writers subscribe.**

Yet some poets are more notable for bringing the movements with which they are associated to perfection — this is true of Alexander Pope, in the eighteenth century, for example. Others straddle two periods, as is the case of W.B.Yeats, the Irish poet who was both a Romantic and a Modernist. Still others are difficult to associate with any movement or school: their voices are so distinctive and seem to defy imitation. John Milton in the seventeenth century, and Gerard Manley Hopkins in the nineteenth century are such writers.

Any poetry, however, may be assimilated to certain stylistic conventions and thematic preoccupations that, together, characterise the main artistic movement of the century to which it belongs. So it is vital to be familiar with these, particularly when we are reading poems from different eras.

The most significant of the aesthetic and thematic divisions in English poetry over the last four hundred years is that between Classicism and Romanticism. In the twentieth century, we are inheritors of the Romantic movement of about two hundred years ago. This momentous phenomenon had many complex features but, above all, it emphasised the importance of personal experience, especially emotion, and the value of such experience in poetry.

Wordsworth's declaration —

> I wandered lonely as a cloud
> That floats on high o'er vales and hills,
> When all at once I saw a crowd,

A host, of golden daffodils

'I Wandered Lonely As a Cloud'

— is Romantic in its emphasis on solitude and on nature, but most importantly it is Romantic in its focus on 'I', the first word of the poem, and repeated in each of its four stanzas.

In spite of a spirited reaction against Romantic principles in the early twentieth century, this concern with personal experience continues to dominate our poetry, even if the settings for these experiences are usually very different from Wordsworth's. Much of the poetry of our time, that is to say, is 'confessional', subjective, self-revelatory — even though, in the best writers, that subjectivity is controlled, elevated and, at times, universalised by associations which take it beyond its immediate subjectivity:

White
Godiva, I unpeel —
Dead hands, dead stringencies.

And now I
Foam to wheat, a glitter of seas.

Sylvia Plath:'Ariel'

Prior to the Romantic and Modern periods, however, in the seventeenth and eighteenth centuries, the emphasis was not, Romantically, on subjectivity, but Classically, on objectivity. This is the principal reason why students of poetry today often find verse from these ages so difficult to read.

In the sonnet sequence, for example — such as those of Sir Philip Sidney and William Shakespeare — the poets delight in displaying the variety of their genius within the conventions of that form, but do not, perhaps, utter a single heartfelt phrase from their own immediate experience. The Romantic imagination, while acknowledging the artistry, laments the impersonality.

In reading poetry from the seventeenth and eighteenth centuries, we need to recognise that the poet's consciousness of his role was primarily, if not ultimately, as a wordsmith, working with a host of different poetic forms, and inspired by the poetry of classical antiquity.

Much of the poetry of these centuries is, in a sense, poetry about poetry — such as John Donne's so-called 'Songs and Sonnets' which, Romantically, we would read as the impassioned outpourings of his promiscuous young manhood, but which, more likely, he intended as a rebuttal of the tired contemporary Petrarchan conventions of love poetry, while still revelling in the largely fictional persona he creates.

Our post-Romantic expectation of 'truth to life' cannot always be satisfied in such writing, where the sincerity may be primarily artistic rather than autobiographical. This is not to say that poets of these periods did not look into their hearts and write, as Sidney's 'muse', or the spirit of his poetry, bids him to do, at the beginning of *Astrophel and Stella*. But that very writing typically transformed the personal experience 'into something rich and strange', in Shakespeare's phrase. The poetry, while having its source in the writer's life, is ornamented and artificial, and we cannot begin to appreciate these great writers unless we are prepared to acknowledge and admire their technical skill and use of literary conventions, which at once beautify and depersonalise their works. The prejudices of our age, which is suspicious of elegance and formality, nonetheless pose formidable obstacles to our reading of this poetry.

THEME

Having set the poem in the context of its author's life and the historical and literary or artistic period to which it belongs, we are equipped in general terms to approach its particular meaning. A poem by a twentieth-century Australian woman, such as Gwen Harwood, belongs to a very different world from that of a later nineteenth-century Englishman, such as Robert Browning. Poetry does not come into existence in a vacuum. As well as being a work of art, each poem is a biographical and historical document.

As well as being a work of art, each poem is a biographical and historical document.

Our first step in approaching a poem's unique meaning is to describe its theme. Too often readers ignore the titles of poems which can be the key both to their meaning and to their style. In the title of Browning's 'Soliloquy of the Spanish Cloister', for example, both the exotic setting and the style — a dramatic monologue — are captured.

That Keats' poem on melancholy is entitled 'Ode' prepares us for a formal celebration:

> Aye, in the very temple of Delight
> Veiled Melancholy has her sov'reign shrine.

Eliot's 'Portrait of a Lady' suggests a detailed character portrayal but with something of the detachment of Henry James,

19

whose novel of the same name it recalls. Gwen Harwood's 'Alter Ego' plainly introduces the theme of another self, the classical title preparing us for the Mozartian parallel she draws.

Subtitles, too, when they are present, are instructive. Coleridge subtitled his poem, 'Kubla Khan', 'a vision in a dream' thus introducing the air of mystery and fancy which prevails in that work.

In presenting a poem's theme, try to be as objective as possible. It is important that a poem means something to you, but in describing its meaning, we need to show how that meaning is available to others also. To this end, such subjective and tentative phrases as 'I think' and 'I feel' should be avoided. Poems present ideas and theses, even arguments about aspects of life. These can and should be expounded as rationally as possible, while we remember that other readers might find different meanings, and that all of these may be distinct from the poet's meaning, which we can never certainly know. What matters is that our interpretation is closely supported by examples from the text.

> **It is important that a poem means something to you, but in describing its meaning, we need to show how that meaning is available to others also.**

In indicating the theme of A.E. Housman's 'Loveliest of Trees, the Cherry Now', we focus initially on that title, taken from the first line, and discern a note of celebration in the superlative — 'loveliest' — and a sense of urgency in 'now'. This is in fact the dual theme of the poem which is a lyrical praise of nature's beauty but also a statement of the poet's sense that time is passing for him and he must enjoy the present moment in its fullness:

> Now, of my threescore years and ten,
> Twenty will not come again.

The poem, thus, is both happy and melancholy, reflecting on the lovely cherry blossom but regretting the transitoriness of human life in which to enjoy it:

> And since to look at things in bloom
> Fifty springs are little room,
> About the woodlands I will go
> To see the cherry hung with snow.

The speaker, in this poem, in other words, has two themes which complement each other.

STYLE

Of all the literary arts, poetry is the most artistically concentrated. Through the use of a vast range of formal devices, poets, from the earliest times, have sought to heighten and intensify their ideas through rhythm, rhyme, metaphor, symbol, the use of structural conventions (as in the lyric, sonnet, elegy, epic and so on) and a host of other features of style.

Having identified the principal theme or themes of a poem, we should turn our attention to stylistic matters to explain the poet's choice of a particular method of writing for his or her subject, and assess its appropriateness. In Housman's poem, to which we referred in the last section, the poet has deliberately chosen a song-like lyrical style, for he wishes to convey his essential happiness in his contemplation of nature. He is in a melodious mood.

It is essential to remember that style, in poetry, is not merely

21

a decoration imposed on meaning. Often students will go through the motions of noting the stylistic features of a poem in the way of a laborious exercise in artistic appreciation distinct from (and subsequent to) describing a poem's theme. Style should illuminate and amplify subject, as in Gwen Harwood's 'Prize-Giving', where the spacious stanzas reflect the formal occasion introduced in the title.

In the best poems, the form and style are perfectly adapted to the ideas of the poet and intimately assist their communication.

When Robert Burns, like Housman, wants to sing of joy he similarly takes on a song-like voice:

> O my luve's like a red, red rose,
> That's newly sprung in June.

> 'A Red, Red Rose'

And he uses a simile for her (introduced by 'like') which emphasises her natural beauty and summer-time loveliness. The idea of the celebration of love is perhaps the simplest and most common in poetry, but these features of Burns' style in this work give it peculiar and memorable power.

Very differently, in John Clare's paraphrase of a psalm 'Lord, Hear My Prayer', the lyricism is given a dark colouring by words that, in various ways, suggest despair:

> My heart is smitten like the grass,
> That withered lies and dead,
> And I, so lost to what I was,
> Forget to eat my bread.
> My voice is groaning all the day,

My bones prick through this skin of clay.

The short 'i' sounds in the verbs, 'smitten', 'withered', 'prick'
and the onomatopoeia in 'groaning' indicate how style can
augment meaning in poetry; these effects suggesting the
speaker's bitterness and pain. Visual, too, is the last line adding
further impact to the aural effects before.

Then, a stylistic device such as alliteration bestows arresting
impact on poetic language, in the spirited opening to a poem:

I caught this morning morning's minion....

G.M. Hopkins: 'The Windhover'

I imagine this midnight moment's forest....

Ted Hughes: 'The Thought-Fox'

In both cases this stylistic device is there not merely because
these poets considered alliteration necessary in a poem, but for
its usefulness in giving vitality to works in which they are
celebrating the vigour of creation. Of course, alliteration is only
truly appreciated if we read the poems aloud.

Style assists theme, in poetry, and as it is part of it, should be
discussed in conjunction with our treatment of a work's subject
matter, not as an additional quantity. For poets, the manner is
as important as the matter in the communication of meaning.

TECHNICAL TERMS

In our account of a poet's artistry, we need to be familiar with various technical terms for devices of rhythm, rhyme, vocabulary, imagery and so forth which poets use. Compendiums of these terms are at once useful and daunting, for while they provide vital information, they seem to require enormous knowledge of difficult and strange learning before we even approach a poem.

Again, in this matter, it is vital to regard the poem itself as the primary document. The more poetry we read, the more often we will come across the use of various techniques by poets to embody their meaning artistically. As we proceed — and this may take some years — we will gather for ourselves a growing knowledge of technical devices and a sense of their importance.

> **The more poetry we read, the more often we will come across the use of various techniques by poets is embody their meaning artistically.**

We have already referred to some of the main types of poems, such as the **Epic**, a narrative work of considerable length dealing with a heroic theme in elevated language. *Paradise Lost*, by Milton, recounting the 'Fall' of humanity and the expulsion of Adam and Eve from the Garden of Eden, is the most famous example in English. But we also need to be familiar with types of **Ballad**, **Satire** (as in the 'mock epic') **Ode**, **Lyric**, **Sonnet** and so on.

We should be able to identify the traditional verse forms. **Blank Verse**, for example, is in the rhythm of speech and not rhymed. It is the principal form for dramatic poetry, as in Shakespeare. Very different is the use of the **Couplet** — a pair of rhyming lines usually strictly rhythmical — which was the dominant style of eighteenth-century verse. The **Quatrain**, with four rhyming lines in various combinations of patterns (such as ABAB), is familiarly found in the fourteen-line sonnet, consisting of three quatrains and a concluding couplet.

Such frameworks are not used for their own sake. They enable poets to structure their arguments and imagery. The division of the sonnet into the eight-line **Octave** and six-line **Sestet** provides a convenient way, for example, of complementing the idea initially introduced with its resolution. The octave/sestet break may also introduce a change in imagery.

Obviously, knowledge about **Rhythm** and familiarity with the terms used to describe it, are vital to our reading and discussion of poetry, which is the rhythmic art of language.

A poetic line usually consists of stressed and unstressed syllables. Where a pattern of these emerges, we can see (or hear) the metre of the poem, and each unit in that pattern is known as a 'foot'. In this line from 'The Rime of the Ancient Mariner' by Coleridge —

U / U / U / U /
The bride hath paced into the hall

— there are four feet. This is the most common arrangement of rhythm in English poetry: an unstressed syllable followed by a stressed one. This is known as **Iambic Metre,** and as there are four feet in that line, it is technically described as **Iambic Tetrameter. Iambic Pentameter** (with five feet) is also very popular in English verse:

$$\cup \quad / \quad \cup \quad / \cup \quad / \quad \cup \quad / \quad \cup \quad /$$
A small house agent's clerk, with one bold stare.

T.S Eliot: *The Waste Land*

When identifying rhythms thus, we must always show why they are appropriate to the poet's subject. In the example of Coleridge, for instance, the even deliberateness of that regular rhythm is very apt for the ceremonious procession of the wedding party, amplified by the stressed participle 'paced'. In Eliot's case, he has used throughout the passage from which that line comes, a careful pattern of alternately rhymed iambic pentameters to give an elevated appearance to what is, in fact, a low occasion. There, the technique is used satirically.

The reverse of the iambic rhythm is the **Trochaic**, where the stress falls on the first syllable of the foot. This is particularly useful for an arresting opening:

$$/ \quad \cup \quad / \cup \quad / \quad \cup \cup / \quad \cup$$
Father, father, where are you going?

William Blake: 'The Little Boy Lost'

Less urgent, but more poignant is the **Dactylic**:

$$/ \quad \cup \quad \cup / \quad \cup \quad / \quad \cup \cup /$$
Death stands above me, whispering low.

W.S.Landor: 'Death Stands Above Me'

We also have, in this one line, personification and onomatopoeia: death seems very near indeed, as a consequence of Landor's accomplished technique.

The identification of metre, known as the 'scansion' of a

poem, is an important aid to the appreciation of the poet's methods of conveying his meaning. And the brief suspension of the rhythmic process, known as the **Caesura**, can be just as effective:

Home is so sad. ‖ It stays as it was left.

Philip Larkin: 'Home is so Sad'

Here, the caesura, like a pause in music, prepares us for the explanation of the sadness and initiates an emotional quality of melancholy in this poem by that very waiting on the next phrase, as in its concluding line:

The music in the piano stool. ‖ That vase.

Again, it is by reading aloud that this device is appreciated.

We also need to be clear about the meanings of such technical terms as **Alliteration** and **Assonance**, **Simile** and **Metaphor**, **Image** and **Symbol** and many others (see Glossary). These will be mastered as we read attentively, come to recognise their presence immediately, and appreciate their value in art and usefulness in literary criticism.

Every student of poetry should possess a study such as *The Anatomy of Poetry* by Marjorie Boulton (Routledge and Kegan Paul: London, revd. ed. 1982) or *Mastering English Literature* by Richard Gill (Macmillan: London, 1985) which deal clearly and thoroughly with these matters.

EVALUATION

With the subject or argument of a poem analysed, with regard to its artistic realisation, we are ready for its evaluation. Simply because poems áre set for study does not mean that they are necessarily good, let alone great. Some poets who were idolised in past centuries are now forgotten, while we may reasonably suppose that some of those in favour today will be neglected in the future.

> **Simply because poems are set for study does not mean that they are necessarily good, let alone great.**

However, if we are to judge a poem, we must make our principles of assessment clear and, particularly, we should be on our guard against rejecting poets from previous ages for their failure to conform with the prejudices of today or writers with fervent beliefs different from ours. To our sceptical and realistic temperaments, the exuberant Romanticism of Keats may seem excessive or ludicrous. Even twentieth-century writers may have concerns that are foreign to us. To the youthful reader, the middle-aged anxieties of Eliot's famous persona, J. Alfred Prufrock, could appear merely satirical; to the atheist, the quest of his Magi is a futile fantasy.

Poetry is the most humane of the arts and should always be enlarging our sympathies. In our assessment of a poem we should strive to be absorbed into its world. Then we are unlikely to judge a poem adversely on the grounds of its subject matter.

Where our evaluation can be valid and incisive, however, is in our commentary on the poet's treatment of the subject in artistic terms — on matters of expression or form. We can debate the wisdom of Blake's choice of the simplistic, song-like form for his poems of social criticism. We might find the cataloguing of mundane elements of life in John Tranter's work insufficiently profound to be resonant. We may wish for more lyricism and less learning from Gwen Harwood. We may find one poem too long, another too short for its subject. But we should never reject a poem on the grounds that we cannot agree or identify with its theme. Everything is susceptible to artistic treatment. Whether or not the treatment is artistic, of course, is the pertinent question for each reader to argue and determine.

LITERARY CRITICISM

Finally, we may consider referring to the published criticism of poetry as a companion to our reading. While some argue that the critics are best avoided and others provide extensive reading lists of secondary material on a writer, there is no hard and fast answer in this matter. The advice, however, that one should try to read at least one thorough critical account of an author who is being carefully read is sound. But the poem and our response to it should always remain the primary focus of our reading.

If we would enrich and enlarge our appreciation, it is all but inevitable that we will need the assistance of scholars who have made detailed studies of the writer's life and work. An authoritative biography or critical examination prevents us from making simple mistakes and misreadings and, more positively, will extend our understanding.

But we have to be careful, especially in the case of writers like T.S.Eliot, where the body of critical work is far larger than his own corpus of poetry, from becoming obsessed with, or oppressed by, the huge amount of interpretative material on his writing.

Poets write not for professional critics, but for readers. The centre of our attention should always be the poem itself. But as intelligent readers, we should welcome the collaboration of others in what Eliot himself described as 'the common pursuit of true judgement'.

29

The Poetry of Emily Dickinson

Birth and Family

Emily Dickinson was born in the tiny community of Amherst, Massachusetts, in the north-eastern United States, in 1830, in a family which (like so many in the New England area) had Puritan origins. Her ancestors had migrated from persecution in England in the seventeenth century to seek religious and political freedom in America.

Their Calvinistic inheritance (a European theological tradition from the Reformation which emphasised salvation through faith alone and predestination to heavenly bliss for a small portion of humanity known as 'the Elect' and damnation for everybody else) gave to the Dickinsons a serious and sober view of life, a dedication to 'good works' (encouraged as the fruits of faith) in their community, a distaste for frivolity, and a repudiation of idleness in their vigorous pursuit of their God-given vocations in this world. Learning, however, was not despised and because of the emphasis in Puritanism on personal salvation, the Dickinsons' tradition included a respect for individuality and even a tolerance of a degree of eccentricity.

Emily's father, Edward, a lawyer by training, was a prominent citizen in Amherst, being bursar of the college founded there by his father. Her mother (after whom Emily was named) deferred to her husband, in the scriptural manner, and (as her daughter noted) did not 'care for thought'. Emily had an older brother Austin and a younger sister Lavinia. Neither sister ever married or left their family home. Austin settled nearby.

This existence, apparently so narrow, close-knit and restricted, was somewhat broadened by a large acquaintance amongst both their extended family and in the collegiate and religious communities of the area for which the Dickinson home was a lively focus.

SCHOOLING AND ADOLESCENCE

Emily attended Amherst Academy and, from eleven to eighteen, Mount Holyoke Female Seminary. The undemanding curriculum for girls at the time posed no difficulty for her, but she was not distinguished as a scholar nor do we associate her, through her writing in adulthood, with conspicuous learning or bookishness. Her best education came from her detached but close observation of life, and — in the Calvinist way — her consideration of its central issues, especially death and the prospect of immortality. Regular church attendance kept her in constant contact with the theological interpretations of human existence, with biblical teachings about it and with the moral code proclaimed in Calvinist hymns. The linguistic style of the hymns and their musicality, indeed, are reflected in her poetry. Yet, again, she kept her distance from Christian commitment. Her family was 'religious', she noted, 'except me'.

RECLUSIVE ADULTHOOD; UNREQUITED LOVE

There is little documented information about Emily's life, after her formal education had ended, although her letters reveal her isolation even in the midst of her family. Commenting on her 'companions', she refers to the 'hills... and the sundown, and a dog large as my-self'. These are better than human beings, she judges, 'because they know, but do not tell'. She enjoyed a kind of literary companionship, however, with 'Keats, and Mr. and Mrs. Browning'.

From inferences in her poetry, it is suspected that Emily suffered from an unrequited love for the Reverend Charles Wadsworth, a Calvinist minister from Philadelphia, whom she may have met in 1854. If this passion did exist, it was hopeless. Wadsworth was married, and in 1862 he left Philadelphia for distant San Francisco.

POEMS SENT TO HIGGINSON

Although for some years before this crisis in her life, Emily had been writing poetry, it was in the months preceding Wadsworth's departure for the west coast, possibly in the torment of her love for him, that her output was most prodigious. The composition of some 300 poems and her uncharacteristically bold gesture of sending them to a journalist, Thomas Wentworth Higginson, for assessment, are perhaps signs of the turbulence of her emotions at this time:

> Are you too deeply occupied to say if my verse is alive? Should you think it breathed, and had you the leisure to tell me, I should feel quick gratitude.

Even allowing for the conventional style of address in a letter in this situation, at that time, we can sense in these words the fragility of Emily's self-confidence, the almost painful tentativeness with which she is reaching out from detachment to connection with the world. Higginson, in response, mixed his critique of her verse with encouraging words and they established a regular correspondence. He did not believe, however, that there was an audience for her poems amongst contemporary readers, although — after her death — he saw the first selection of them through the press.

HER LAST YEARS

Committed totally to her vocation as a poet, Emily became completely reclusive. Any who would visit her had to communicate with her through her sister Lavinia. She dressed only in white, and this 'habit', as it were, and her 'enclosed' existence, so to speak, led to the description of her as 'the nun of Amherst'. But Emily was more isolated than a nun — who belongs, even in an enclosed order, to a community of religious sisters. She was more like an anchoress, secluded for meditation on the profound truths of life. Yet, however narrow her personal circumstances, her poetry opens out to the world, the great drama of human experience and its fundamental questions.

Emily's father and mother pre-deceased her, in 1874 and 1882 respectively. She died before both her brother and sister, however, in May 1886, from kidney degeneration.

DICKINSON'S LITERARY IMPORTANCE

Dickinson is an important poet principally because of the distinctiveness of her writing. Critics have compared her, in this way, to a contemporary English poet (unknown to her), Gerard Manley Hopkins. Their styles are utterly different, but both write without any substantial evidence of influence upon the formation and evolution of their styles and themes, from any 'school' of poetry; and, because of their peculiarities, both have proved to be inimitable. Dickinson's singularity of style and themes is the essence of her achievement.

To characterise it, however, we are able to compare her writing with some other well-known poets. In her use of religious idioms and references, in her lyricism and her persistent preoccupation with the issues of mortality and eternity, she is reminiscent of the seventeenth-century English poet, George Herbert — though she certainly did not share his orthodox Christianity. In her despair and desolation, with their subtext of disappointment in love and human relationships, and the sense that her poems give of speaking directly out of her tragedy, she also looks forward to Stevie Smith, a twentieth-century English poet. But Stevie Smith has little of Dickinson's consummate technical artistry and restraint which, unaffectedly but beautifully, presents complex and subtle ideas and states of mind and emotion, with a disarming simplicity.

It is extraordinary, given the restricted character of Dickinson's life, that she could write so profoundly and powerfully about the human condition. Or perhaps it is by virtue of that very seclusion that she had the time and circumstances in which to meditate and to create. Yet, it seems that it was a decidedly worldly and familiar event —an unhappy love for another — that concentrated her artistry.

Dickinson, for all her distinctiveness, is one of the poets of unhappiness — her contemporary, Christina Rossetti, is another. But her genius is that she gives artistic status to her personal suffering: she is never morbid or maudlin. The sweet lyricism of her musical voice is combined with a strength of thought, a range of imagery, a variety of vocabulary and a profundity of experience to produce poetry that is at once peculiarly her own and of universal significance.

THE POEMS

There's a certain slant of light

The experience of melancholy is presented here in a poetry that, stylistically, has a crisp, terse quality. Dickinson does not diminish her knowledge of 'despair' by indulging in self-pity, or by writing in lugubrious language. There is, instead, objectivity and detachment in the impersonality of the speaker ('we' not 'I') — which also gives universality to the poem's meaning — and in the use of extended imagery from nature, which reinforces the general application of the subject to the world and the idea that this affliction is at the heart of its being.

The setting of the lyric, in the opening stanza, is apparently most striking in the short second line, 'Winter afternoons', which establishes the ideas of death and decline (and we need to remember the harshness of a Massachusetts winter). However, on re-reading, the conventionality of this imagery becomes less significant than the opening subtlety of description — 'a certain slant of light'. The 'slant' suggests something awry — a perversion in creation, as well as the more obvious indication of light being seen from an oblique angle (and, perhaps, even more accurately, from that angle). That it is 'light', furthermore, which is disturbing, is also striking, for customarily light is associated with warmth, hope, even God's presence.

Light as it is seen here, however

> oppresses like the heft
> Of cathedral tunes.

Again, Dickinson is contradicting expectation in this simile. For light, adjectivally, is conceived of as weightless, yet that heavy verb, 'oppresses', and the blunt 'heft' (or 'weight') show that this slant of light is entirely different in its effect from light as it is usually experienced. That its burdensome quality should be like the resonant sound of cathedral music, ascribes to it a religious portentousness that is not consoling, but oppressive. With a stylistic irony, Dickinson is writing of such heaviness in a poetry that is itself mostly light and lyrical in manner.

This slant of light is peculiar, to be differentiated from ordinary light, in its 'certain' particularity. And in the second stanza, Dickinson indicates precisely its theological significance. With her Calvinist Puritan background, she is referring both to the idea of Original Sin and the punishment of alienation from God ('Heavenly hurt') which was its consequence. We have but one 'scar', which is not like an external, physical wound, but the soul's affliction which has profoundly separated us from heaven — 'internal difference'. And this is the explanation of the human condition, the elucidation of its tragedy: 'where the meanings are'.

Where Dickinson is to be separated, however, from Calvinist teaching is in the absence of a theology of salvation to compensate for this judgment. Indeed, she deliberately uses the word 'despair' — not only for its emotional impact as representative of an experience of profound desolation, but for its precise theological meaning as the most grave of sins: the conviction that there can be no salvation from our mortality, no resurrection from death.

This concentration on a 'slant of light', that is to say, reveals Heaven's purposes as indifferent to the present condition of humanity:

> None may teach it any...

as being irreversible in their consequences:

> 'Tis the seal despair...

and imposed magisterially (with the implication of 'unjustifiably')
from on high:

> An imperial affliction
> Sent us of the air.

For all its insubstantial character, Dickinson is far from denying
the light's overwhelming impact — not only in human lives, but
in the creation at large:

> When it comes the landscape listens,
> Shadows hold their breath.

Nature here is personified to establish its connection with
humanity (and ours with it) in this affliction.

The closing lines —

> When it goes 'tis like the distance
> On the look of death

— release to a degree the tension that has been accumulating
through the stanzas, but they do not relax the poem into
consolation. The departure of the light is not absolute, as the
poet's simile indicates. What this light represents is always

present, though it may be removed, at a 'distance', from us. And what it signifies is the essential truth about all life — that it is touched by and will be consumed in death. Dickinson is suggesting here, in writing of miraculously poised ambiguity, that the 'slant of light' stands for a phenomenon that is at once at the heart of our being (our mortality — the scar within) and that yet seems so strange to us, as we pursue our ordinary existences. The 'look of death', so distant from us, is in essence what we are.

Focus Question

How does Emily Dickinson universalise her personal sense of despair in this poem?

I felt a funeral in my brain

A meditation on death, this poem derives its unique force from the dream (or nightmare)-like quality of its narrative and the tormented individuality of the speaker's experience. The surreal quality of the recollection is established in the opening line:

> I felt a funeral in my brain

as the verb (to feel) is strikingly original in its apparent inappropriateness to a mental vision. Its purpose, of course, is to introduce the immediacy of the idea, which has engaged not only her thoughts but her feelings as well — her whole being. The alliteration on 'f' binds the verb and the noun in an arresting combination. What is more, the 'funeral' that she feels is portrayed in active terms:

> And mourners to and fro.

This is not a static undertaking, but determined and, what is more, threatening — a frightening persistence poetically enacted in enjambement:

> to and fro
> Kept treading....

The repetition of 'treading' aurally brings this spectral scene to life with a peculiarly oppressive pounding that is at once violent and pregnant with meaning:

> till it seemed
> That sense was breaking through.

In her art of ambiguity, Dickinson suggests — in 'breaking through' — both the positive revelation of meaning and the disturbing abruptness of the encounter with truth. She is focusing, in other words, on the centrality of death in life. If she can understand the concept, all will be set in order in her mind. However, that very 'sense' might be so maddening as to destroy her very being.

The narrative of the funeral continuing, the speaker echoes the 'treading, treading' of the first stanza, with 'beating, beating' in the second. This rhythmical stress governs the hymn-like arrangement of this lyric. Ironically, although the poem is thus indebted to Emily Dickinson's experience of worship in church, it articulates a critique of liturgy:

> till I thought
> My mind was going numb.

Most profoundly, however, she is sustaining (and deepening), in this stanza, the sense of being haunted by the implications of the mortal event conceived in her imagination, even as she now registers her inability to be receptive to its significance.

The repetition of 'And', which grows in insistent replication as the poem proceeds, has a biblical quality. Dickinson is conveying the divinely-ordained character of death, as well as (in apparent antithesis) its ugly physical brutality:

> With those same boots of lead again....

She is also indicating how the human rendition of spiritual truth, in dogma and church practices, can trample on its subtleties.

Onomatopoeia brings the conception immediately to our senses here, in 'creak' and 'toll', and the sounds, in their unattractiveness, contribute to the evaluation of the occasion.

We notice how the worlds of reality and spirituality are discomfortingly merged in this writing. The tactile 'box' — that is, a coffin — and the aural 'creak' of the pallbearers' tread pass across her soul; and the bell-like tolling of funereal custom is performed by airy 'space'. The speaker is discovered, in other words, in a kind of trance where the ordinary distinctions of nature and the supernatural are dissolved. Characteristically, for Dickinson, this is not an inspiring experience, but desolating.

In the fourth stanza, the dimensional confusion of the physical and the metaphysical is elaborated in the surprising spatial reduction of the 'Heavens' to 'a bell' and 'being' to 'an ear', which also concentrates, visually, and clarifies, argumentatively, the poet's theme: all of human creation, as the 17th century poet, John Donne argued, is summoned to its essential destiny when the bell tolls.

Yet the speaker separates herself, is estranged from this universal call. As the drum-like service, earlier, had numbed her, so now she, and silence, do not hear the bell of Heaven, and cannot respond to it. They are like

> some strange race
> Wrecked solitary here.

Yet, in conclusion, Dickinson appears to reject what she has just despairingly affirmed. She imagines her own submission to eternity in a vision of damnation:

And I dropped down and down
And hit a world at every plunge,
And finished knowing then.

This is at the cost of what she values most highly:

And then a plank in reason broke.

The resistance of human knowledge to the persuasion of faith, in the ultimate matters of death and immortality, is being explored in this poem in the context of a critique that surely derives from Dickinson's first-hand, familial experience of Calvinistic Puritanism, where intellectual reservations were worn down by theological insistence.

Nonetheless, she appears to concede in the last line that beyond reason — that is, after our human lives — there will be an ultimate explanation of being, superior to our worldly intellectuality or 'knowing'. 'Finished', here, means not only 'ended up', but 'stopped'. In the second meaning, it is again ironic in effect, for the speaker is suggesting that the eternal condition beyond death is a state of oblivion, rather than revelation. Unlike her Christian brethren, she does not imagine that, in God's presence, she will know even as she is known.

That this state is reached so violently — 'and hit a world at every plunge' — presents it also as a place of punishment.

'I felt a funeral in my brain' is the poem of a writer haunted by mortality who is able, nevertheless, to give that very familiar anxiety an idiosyncratic artistic expression, dramatising the torment of her preoccupation.

Focus Question

How does Dickinson make the familiar ceremonies of a funeral so vivid in this poem?

I dreaded that first robin so

In presenting a series of nature's beauties, in creatures and plants, the speaker explores her alienation from the fertile and regenerating powers of life in this poetic drama of her despair of love. The dramatic disposition of the writing is introduced in the forcefulness of 'dreaded' — which is a powerful word in any context, but especially when the object of dread is something as harmless and pretty as the robin. But that is Dickinson's point. So extreme is her despair that even the slightest sign of new life and hope accentuates her grief. Consequently, the robin, now seen and heard, has had to be 'mastered', though the mastery is incomplete:

> I'm some accustomed to him grown —
> He hurts a little, though.

The American quality of the poet's language, incidentally, is very apparent here in the colloquial abbreviation of 'somewhat'.

The sense of Dickinson's fragile survival, given the agony of her endurance of life's trials, is perfectly enacted in the language of the next line:

> I thought if I could only live

— in the tentativeness of 'I thought', the contingency of 'if', the desperation of 'I could only live'. The robin's song is amplified, almost humorously (but it is a black comedy), to a 'shout'. If she could survive it, then she might feel confident in enduring all of nature's music:

> Not all pianos in the woods
> Had power to mangle me.

We are struck, in this poem, as in 'I felt a funeral in my brain', by the vivid immediacy of the speaker's evocation of physical violence to her body: 'hurts' in the first stanza, 'mangle' here, and 'pierce' in the next, as a metaphor for her spiritual suffering. Some readers will discern a foretaste of Sylvia Plath's poetry wherein metaphysical pain is presented with a lacerating physicality.

The distant alliteration of 'dared' with 'dreaded' yet sustains the extremity of the speaker's condition and the deathly colouring of her mood. And it is ironic that this device should be extended, next, to the lovely daffodils, whose

> yellow gown
> Would pierce me with a fashion
> So foreign to my own.

She is referring here, in this visual imagery of detachment, to her black robe of mourning, representative of the wintry world to which she has been permanently consigned, so different from the bright attire of spring.

In contrast, in the fourth stanza, the speaker now pleads for the quickening of nature's processes: 'I wished the grass would hurry', but in order that she might be hidden by it. Then the tallest grass, searching for her above, would miss her below:

> He'd be too tall, the tallest one
> Could stretch to look at me.

Again (particularly in 'stretch', with its implication of strain), there is the idea of the lack of reciprocity between the speaker and creation — her awkward and painful dissociation from its motivation and processes.

In striking alliteration, once more, the bees are negatively perceived in her observation that she 'could not bear' them, with the sense, again, in the verb, of the burden of even the lightest of nature's beings:

> I wished they'd stay away
> In those dim countries where they go.
> What word had they for me?

The rhetorical question emphasises that this is the writing of one who is utterly separated from the hope of love, and who is also taunted and tormented by the springtime rebirth of the world:

> They're here though; not a creature failed.

She remembers that Easter (in the northern hemisphere) occurs in this season, and, in a grim irony, her self-dramatisation reaches its climax as her suffering unto death, a sacrifice of Christ-like implications for her own being, takes place, cruelly, in a world of abundant fertility and beauty:

> No blossom stayed away
> In gentle deference to me,
> The Queen of Calvary.

All who are now present, personified, ceremoniously acknowledge her. But they are in ignorance of the significance of her suffering, even of its existence —'their unthinking drums' —

in their ritual of hail and farewell. Dickinson intensifies the comparison with the crucified Jesus, now modulating, in these martial details, reminiscent of the Roman soldiery, of salutes and drums, and the 'plumes' she wears, to the concept of an imperial military triumph. That her ornamentation is 'childish' suggests, at the poem's close, a self-criticism of her former tragic perception of herself, culminating in its aggrandisement in the description of herself as 'The Queen of Calvary'. Plumage is associated with pride, and we sense that this writer, who so often speaks of her detachment from life, has attained, in this closing stanza, something of a wry detachment from herself and her experience of bereavement — that is, the loss of the Reverend Charles Wadsworth to San Francisco. If so, this poem enacts the therapeutic function to which many poets have referred: by writing about her pain, Dickinson seems to have come to terms with it and, through accumulating exaggeration to the point of absurdity, learnt to a degree to separate herself from it and, so, to alleviate it.

Nonetheless, the abiding impression which the reader has of the experience recounted here is of the speaker's alienation from all creation.

Focus Question

What is your assessment of the poet's description of herself as 'The Queen of Calvary' in the context of your reading of the poem as a whole?

48

I heard a fly buzz when I died

Emily Dickinson's preoccupation with death and the after-life, central to the Calvinistic Puritanism in which she was raised (but the tenets of which she could not accept) is given strange artistic formulation in this lyric, where the momentous instant of death, when the Christian hopes to cross from this temporal and mortal world to the eternal, is mockingly diminished, in the very first line:

> I heard a fly buzz when I died.

That she is imaginatively presenting an event that has yet to happen as completed, in the past tense, conveys the certainty of her rejection of the theological interpretation of the occasion of death. That it should be a fly she hears — and its buzzing is onomatopoeically present to reinforce the point — touches her scepticism with comedy.

The arrangement of the poem is extraordinarily skilful, for all the apparent simplicity of its organisation. The opening line is followed by the evocation of the moments just before the fly's buzz, at the point of her death. So while there is no suspense in the narrative — it has been completed, just as the poem starts — all the details that follow, have their religious solemnity queered by that buzzing insect:

> The stillness in the room
> Was like the stillness in the air
> Between the heaves of storm.

The stillness of a calm between a storm's ragings is a portent of the divine. She imagines those around her deathbed (in traditional

Christianity, a profound event, earnestly and keenly attended by the devout, for revelations of God's workings with the dying), their eyes no longer weeping with grief, but zealously watching, and their breathing intensifying,

> For that last onset when the king
> Be witnessed in the room.

They would be alert to Christ's presence as he takes the soul of the dead one into his keeping.

At her farewell, she disposes of her property and her physicality — all that belongs to this world:

> I willed my keepsakes, signed away
> What portion of me be
> Assignable....

And the beginning of the poem is recalled:

> and then it was
> There interposed a fly.

The shock of the opening line is now augmented by the ingredient of bathos in the wake of the pious implications of the events that have been recounted in between. This has the function, yet again, of emphasising Dickinson's detachment from other people's experiences and expectations.

Also described now is the character of the fly's buzz, that had been initially introduced. Oddly, Dickinson colours its sound, in the way of her mixture of senses which we have seen elsewhere:

> With blue uncertain stumbling buzz

which suggests, perhaps, its difference from the brightness of light and the blackness of death's darkness. It is an everyday colour and the sound is unceremonious, bumbling: 'uncertain stumbling'. If this is what death is like, then it could not be more different from the awful occasion described in theology and spirituality.

The fly intervenes between 'the light and me'. This plainly physical writing is also metaphysical. The unprepossessing insect, representative of life at its most ordinary, prevents her encounter with God. Dickinson is suggesting that all she has observed of life contradicts (or, at least, obscures) everything that she has been told about its divine purpose and destiny. The poem closes in complete negativity, in rejection of the light:

> And then the windows failed; and then
> I could not see to see.

The tone here, however, is ambiguous. For all the apparent assurance (even mocking self-confidence) of her conviction that she knows what it will be like at death, there is also an element of frustration and regret in the failing of the windows and her blindness at the end. Could she be lamenting that it is her unique tragedy that, while others see God's face when they die, she hears only a fly buzz? Or is she using her own imagined experience as a warning to those others who subscribe to such supernatural and, on earth, unverifiable teachings?

Focus Question

How would you describe the different tones of this poem?

It was not death, for I stood up

Dickinson presents, in this poem, her experience of death-in-life, to the point of the denial of her very existence. Her being, as she describes it, is at once like that of the dead, yet she is alive:

> It was not death, for I stood up

— and dead ones lie down. It is not of the night, with its connotations of mystery and darkness, for the bells, in grotesque personification,

> Put out their tongues for noon.

Nor is she cold like frost, for warm winds, in a repulsive verb, 'crawl' across her flesh. Yet she is not on fire, but cool with 'marble feet', at once fleshly but disturbingly stony. That they could 'keep a chancel cool', in the midst of these disturbing allusions, beautifully evokes the coolness of that often marbled section of a church. However, the experience she is describing, the 'it' of the opening word, is the combination of all of these contrarieties and their variety of connotations, mediated (as so often in her writing) in vivid sensual terms:

> And yet it tasted like them all.

Observing others laid out for burial. she is reminded by their corpses of her living body. Her being has been shorn of its life-force and, paradoxically, it has been circumscribed by her very existence, imprisoned:

> As if my life were shaven
> And fitted to a frame
> And could not breathe without a key....

Bound to time, her sense is nonetheless of her presence in the oblivion of timelessness:

> And 'twas like midnight some.

But there is no idea of liberation here; rather of stupefying stasis:

> When everything that ticked has stopped
> And space stares all around

— conveyed in the juxtaposition of the onomatopoeic 'ticked' and the abrupt 'stopped', and the terrifying, watching emptiness of boundless space.

Her being, in the penultimate simile, is like a grisly frost, early in Autumn. Covering the living ('beating') earth, annulling (or 'repealing') it, turning its life-force to nothingness.

And, in the last, climactic simile, her experience is

> most like chaos — stopless, cool,
> Without a chance or spar,
> Or even a report of land
> To justify despair.

Dickinson's hopelessness, here, is absolute. She is like one tempest-tossed in the sea, without the prospect of salvation ('a chance') in the sight of a ship's mast (or 'spar'), or even the suggestion of land, to give meaning to her despairing of a safe arrival.

This is nihilism — a scepticism that denies all existence, an even more desperate condition than despair itself, which at least retreats from the concept of the remedy it is rejecting. In theological terms, the 'report of land' would be the scriptural promises to lost souls. But in the poet's experience of harrowing self-knowledge, she is untouched by that good news which could give meaning to her despair.

More specifically biblical is Dickinson's reference to chaos. She is placing her condition here in the state of existence prior to God's creation of the world, which gave form, meaning and purpose to it. That creation was *ex nihilo*, out of nothingness, and this is the state of non-being to which she compares her life. It is the ultimate negation of existence.

Focus Question

How does Dickinson combine her sense of hopelessness with the processes of nature and creation?

I had been hungry all the years

In this subdued and exquisite lyric, with its extended gastronomic metaphor, Dickinson's writing is distantly evocative of a biblical parable and more immediately reminiscent of the religious poetry of George Herbert, the seventeenth century metaphysical lyricist. The simple process of dining, elegantly elaborated to suggest a feast, with 'wine' and 'ample' bread', is a metaphor for a fulfilling life — for example, in the pursuit and attainment of love. But its point here is to emphasise the speaker's estrangement from such fulfilment. She is one accustomed to a lean diet, even hunger.

The sense of Dickinson's deprivation is doubly stressed in the opening line:

> I had been hungry all the years

as the extremity of hunger is coupled with the extended temporal period of 'all the years', suggesting that this had been her condition from birth.

That her turn to 'dine' (with its suggestion not merely of eating to assuage hunger, but to satiate all appetite, as in the fullness of passion) has come at 'noon', indicates the midpoint of her human span, by the reference to the midpoint of day. This is surely a reference to her experience of the possibility of love, in her early thirties.

So different is this sensation from all she has known before that she approaches it with extreme tentativeness:

> I trembling drew the table near
> And touched the curious wine.

We note that, at this stage at least, in this poem, there is neither eating nor drinking. Merely to be in the presence of this strange bounty is sufficiently sensational for her.

In a poignant emblem of her dissociation from the rites of human intercourse, she remembers how hopelessly, in the past, she had looked from the outside, upon the love feasts of others:

> I looked in windows for the wealth
> I could not hope for mine.

Now that she is confronted with such abundance, she remains dumbfounded before it:

> I did not know the ample bread.

Her customary diet is natural ('in nature's dining room') — that is, she accepted the meagre cuisine of her earlier years as her lot, and it came to suit her constitution, as birds will subsist on crumbs.

At the heart of the poem, in other words, is a provocative ambiguity. Tantalising as the feast before her is, and seductive as she has found it in seeing others, from a distance, indulging their appetites, now that she has the opportunity similarly to partake, she curiously finds the repast unappetising. Consciously or not, Dickinson is presenting a psychological dilemma here. Extensive deprivation of sensual satisfaction can at once lead to an obsessive yearning for that satiety and an incapacity to enjoy it when the opportunity presents itself:

> The plenty hurt me, 'twas so new.
> Myself felt ill and odd,
> As berry of a mountain bush
> Transplanted to the road.

That simile of displacement is to be linked with the earlier reflections on her isolation from relationships. The secluded mountain bush would stand little chance of survival by the busy road. So, with the suggestion of an oxymoron, she is hurt by plenty — the communion of life's banquet, dearly sought, has, in reality, proved painful. We should notice here the subtext of religious practice, so often encountered in Dickinson's poetry. Her reference to bread and wine recalls the sacrament of holy communion, and, once again, we note her negative interpretation of religious experience in this allusion, her detachment from it.

Deterministically, she concludes that hers is a negative way. Presented with life's abundance (as in passionate love), she suddenly loses her appetite and prefers the hunger of her accustomed mode of being. That hunger defines her — and all outsiders ('persons outside windows'). Tragically, they imagine that it can be cured by entering into life's fullness, but they are called to an asceticism of the emotions. Should they come to the love-feast, they are both dissociated from their true being and unable to partake: 'the entering takes away', and gives nothing to fill the void that is thus created, for they cannot consume the banquet before them, conditioned as they are to deprivation.

It is possible that Dickinson is using this profound, yet superficially simple analysis of her experience as a means of allaying her distress at her unrequited and impossible love for

Wadsworth. In that case, the bread and wine were not offered to her. She is arguing here that, even if they had been, she would not have had the capacity to consume them.

F ocus Question

Why is the gastronomic metaphor so appropriate to the emotional and spiritual states of the speaker presented in this poem?

I years had been from home

The disposition of this poem is anecdotal and dramatic. The reader is placed in the midst of the occasion in the opening lines, by the emphasis on 'now' and the suspense of the speaker's position 'before the door'. This apprehension is figured stylistically in the enjambe ment of the first and second stanzas:

> lest a face
> I never saw before
>
> Stare stolid into mine
> And ask my business there.

There is a breathlessness in the impetus of those lines which matches her anxiety on the doorstep. Further, the use of repetition, with emphasis — 'My business but a life I left' — gives an insistent quality to her mission and query:

> Was such remaining there?

The poem is set in the context of the narrative of one who has left her home (symbolic of her true setting and vocation in life, the seat of her affections) and, returning, wonders if she might resume what she had earlier spurned. As is often the case in Dickinson's poetry, this simplicity of reference has metaphysical resonance. 'Home' represents both the expectations of her earliest years and the former life she had led (perhaps prior to the irruption of her passion for Wadsworth); and her absence, subsequently, stands for her increasing separation from the fulfilment of that destiny and/or the destabilisation of her ordinary existence by that love.

Ironically, the anecdote here suggests that the speaker has

travelled far, whereas Dickinson, of course, never left home: but she did so metaphysically. The point is very important in our reading of her poetry as a whole — she can convey the sense and experience of a variety of facets of life, for all her reclusive existence; imaginatively entering into its multifariousness and finding metaphors for the complexities of her thoughts and emotions in far-ranging observation.

So estranged is she from her former self that she may be unrecognisable even to those living at the home to which she has returned. The 'face', indeed, who finds her so alien may be her very own. Yet, we might expect — in a religious parable, for example — that, for all her fears of rejection, the anecdote will conclude with the embrace of the absent family member in feasting and rejoicing. But Dickinson was not disposed to such facile optimism. In the third stanza, she ponders her home, her forsaken life, not with affection, but detached 'awe', and, much more powerfully, she hears the accents of her subsequent existence, ambiguously evaluated — like an ocean, crashing against her. She affects to be undaunted by the door, still closed before her and representing the mental and spiritual process that will enable her to remember how life once was, and resume it. The imagery of the closed door and the necessity for it to be opened, for salvation, is biblical.

She is one, after all, who has courageously endured life's trials — one

> Who consternation compassed
> And never winced before

but her spirit fails before this ultimate challenge, nothing less than the revaluation of her whole life, the rejection of the 'second life' of passion, and the resumption of her reclusive existence.

As the action of the poem's drama reaches its climax,

> I fitted to the latch
> My hand with trembling care,
> Lest back the awful door should spring
> And leave me in the floor....

But she cannot enter:

> and like a thief
> Fled gasping from the house.

That last onomatopoeic participle, 'gasping', is terrifyingly immediate in its aurally and visually dramatic presentation of someone appalled by her recognition of the tragedy of her life. We notice how 'home' of the first line has become 'the house' of the last. That change is an emblem of the speaker's utter detachment from consolation, and testimony, once more, to the subtle genius of Dickinson's art of simplicity.

Focus Question
How would you account for the use of the last two similes in the poem ?

Because I could not stop for Death

The central concerns of Dickinson's poetry, death and immortality, are directly named and weighed in this lyric. Like so many poets before her, she personifies Death, but somewhat unusually presents him as a courteous gentleman. In particular, we notice that his courtesy is kindness. Like Stevie Smith, an English poet of this century, Dickinson looks on Death almost as a lover, gladly welcomed. The release from life which Death affords is a blessing, especially as he is accompanied by 'immortality'.

She had introduced herself as one who 'could not stop', with the sense of the constant activity which characterises life with its feverish diversions from the concentration on its ultimate destiny. Death, she notices with relief, both stops and moves calmly and slowly. His dispensation of graciousness she would gladly accept:

> We slowly drove. He knew no haste,
> And I had put away
> My labour and my leisure too
> For his civility.

The alliteration of 'labour' and 'leisure' combines those opposites to dismiss them in a conjunction. In this world, both work and pleasure are strenuously pursued, and are ultimately demeaning.

Everything on earth is active: children do not merely play, but are striving, as she views them — but in futility, 'in the ring'. The grain, seen to be 'gazing', conveys the sense of wide-eyed stupidity, and whether we pass the sun or he passes us, is inconsequential once the world of eternity has been entered. The incantatory repetition of 'passed' emphasises her willed detachment from mortality: it has been superseded.

Her engagement with the world is fraught with the idea of its uncomfortable unpleasantness. Although she is beautifully attired, nature is too cold and damp, and she would be free from its assaults:

> The dews drew quivering and chill.
> For only gossamer my gown,
> My tippet only tulle.

The very sounds of 'quivering' and 'chill' send a shiver through the reader, too.

The house that they pause before, on their progress to eternity, is surrealistically presented with only its roof above ground. Is this a foretaste of the house of death, or an emblem of the disappearance of her domestic world?

The protracted tedium of her life, as she meditates on this encounter with Death and immortality, is poetically exaggerated as 'centuries', to describe this experience she had in her past. But it is also an event that haunts her with a daily immediacy, as if it had happened earlier in the same day. It is Dickinson's way of indicating what so many of her poems reveal: that she was perpetually beset by the idea of Death and the prospect of eternity. This poem in particular, however, is noteworthy for the very pleasant picture she presents of the courteous company of Death.

Focus Question

What is the significance of the use of various movements (driving slowly, passing, pausing...) in this poem?

EXAMINATION-STYLE QUESTIONS WITH GUIDELINES

IMPORTANT: In all discussion of poetry, whether in conversation or writing, it is essential that we support every statement we make about a poem — its subject matter or its style — with examples from the text, noting both **what** is said, and **how** it is said.

All quotations from the poetry **must** be word-perfect.

1. 'That in Dickinson's *Selected Poems* more poems begin with "I" than any other word, indicates that her writing is so self-obsessed as to fail to communicate universal human experiences.' Do you agree?

• Choose two or three of the set poems that begin with 'I' and decide whether or not you agree with the proposition.

• In 'I felt a funeral in my brain', for example, the experience described is certainly uniquely the poet's own. But the concern with death and its meaning is a universal preoccupation.

• Consider the imagery in this poem — is it so odd as to make the experience private, rather than public?

• In 'I dreaded that first robin so', for example, the individual sense of extreme personal suffering, while vividly presented, touches also on everyone's sense, at some stage in their lives, of alienation from the world.

- Consider the sequence of allusions and images in this poem — how they enable the poetry to expand from personal experience to the world at large.

2.   'It is Dickinson's unusual and arresting visual sense that makes her poetry so original and striking'. Discuss.

- Choose two or three of the set poems where you have been particularly struck by the peculiarities of the descriptive writing.

- In 'There's a certain slant of light', for example, we are invited, at the beginning of the poem, to picture the weak winter light which seems to present a critique of and a judgment upon life.

- The physical qualities of the light perfectly match the argument of the poem about our doom-laden condition.

- In 'I heard a fly buzz when I died', for example, the eerie setting of the deathbed and the appearance and motions of the fly, combine visually the variously solemn and detached ideas of death and its circumstances that Dickinson is examining here.

- Once the surprise (even shock) of such writing has abated does it retain its interest?

3. 'Essentially, Dickinson is a religious poet, though her poems present a sustained critique and rejection of Christian teaching'. Do you agree?

- Choose two or three of the set poems where theological matters are raised and the poet distances herself from the orthodox solutions to them .

- In 'It was not death, for I stood up', for example, Dickinson considers the experience of life and her sense of detachment from it, concluding that all is meaningless chaos — thus implicitly rejecting the Christian idea of a benevolent, omniscient God. The poem is nihilistic in argument.

- Show how Dickinson presents her spiritual desolation here in immediately physical terms.

- In 'I had been hungry all the years', for example, Dickinson refers both implicitly and explicitly to the deprivation of the spirit in human life in general (in the failure of love) and religious life in particular (in her inability to taste the bread and wine).

- Very often, she will introduce Christian ideas and practices, but always she registers her dissociation from them — especially the consolation they propose for the tragedy and mortality of existence.

4. 'As a lyrical poet, Dickinson is a consummate singer, but her songs are weighed down by the sadness of their themes'. Do you agre e?

- Choose two or three of the set poems to evaluate the style of Dickinson's writing and to determine whether this observation is accurate.

- In 'I years had been from home', for example, there is an easy rhythm and a regular rhyme. The poem is deceptively 'light' in style, but the experience described is devastating.

- Isn't it the case that that very discrepancy is apt? By the light touch of lyricism, the tragedy of the situation is not diminished, but is given a dramatic immediacy.

- In 'Because I could not stop for Death', for example, the idea of a courtship by Death of the singer is decidedly lyrical, in the context of the rhyme and rhythm here. And such writing is also appropriate to the sense of movement — of a progress to eternity — in this poem.

- Again, the sadness that is present does not sit oddly with the lyricism. Rather, that unhappiness is contained and, in a sense, purified by the chastity of style.

Special Assignment

Consider all the poems of Emily Dickinson that have been set for study. Do you agree that there are qualities about them that make it clear that they were written by a woman, or do you disagree? Explain your response.

GLOSSARY OF LITERARY TERMS

This list includes and defines several of the most commonly mentioned stylistic features of poetry.

ALLITERATION a method of emphasis where words with the same initial consonant are found in close proximity, for cumulative effect:

O _w_ild _W_est _W_ind, thou breath of Autumn's being....

(P.B.Shelley: 'Ode to the West Wind')

ASSONANCE the repetition of vowel sounds:

Such weight and th_i_ck p_i_nk bulk....

(Ted Hughes: 'View of a Pig')

BALLAD a narrative poem, telling a simple story of love, war or adventure, with a brisk rhythm and a regular rhyme, e.g. John Keats' 'La Belle Dame sans Merci'.

BLANK VERSE unrhymed iambic pentameter (see under METRE below), which has been a favourite form in English for dramatic writing as it represents the rhythms of ordinary speech, e.g. in Shakespeare's plays.

CAESURA a break in a poetic line causing a pause in the rhythm:

I sit in the top of the tree, ‖ my eyes closed.

(Ted Hughes: 'Hawk Roosting')

CONFESSIONAL POETRY frank description of personal experiences, including family problems and the poet's mental and emotional life, as found in much modern poetry, e.g. Robert Lowell's *Life Studies*.

COUPLET   a sequence of two rhymed lines, often rhythmically identical too:

Then flashed the living lightning from her eyes,

And screams of horror rend the affrighted skies.

(Alexander Pope: *The Rape of the Lock*, III)

ELEGY   a poem of mourning for the dead.

ENJAMBEMENT   occurs when the sense and rhythm of a poetic line is carried on into the next line:

The tide is full, the moon lies fair
Upon the straits.

(Matthew Arnold: 'Dover Beach')

EPIC   a long poem, recounting a great story of heroic deeds in an elevated language, e.g. John Milton's *Paradise Lost*.

IMAGE   a figure of speech or of descriptive writing which, through comparing the subject to something else, increases understanding of it. In 'The Lake Isle of Innisfree', W.B. Yeats presents the island as an image of peace and contemplation.

LYRIC   a general term for the shortest poems, but deriving from the idea of poetry being written to be set to music and sung.

METAPHOR   used to refer to one thing in terms of another. In 'The Road Not Taken', Robert Frost uses the two roads metaphorically: one standing for the populous way of ordinary existence, the other 'less travelled by' — a metaphor for the lonelier life of the artist.

METRE   the repetitive pattern of rhythm or stresses in poetry. This sign / is used above a syllable or word that is stressed; this ∪ indicates an unstressed syllable. Very common in poetry is the unstressed followed by the stressed: ∪ / — an iambic foot. Iambic pentameter, five iambic feet in a line, is the most common in English poetry:

∪ /   ∪ / ∪ / ∪ / ∪ /

Of showers and sunshine, as of man's desires
   (Alexander Pope: *An Essay on Man*)

ODE a formal poem of commemoration, e.g. John Keats' Odes.

ONOMATOPOEIA where sounds of words imitate or mime the sound being described:

The redbreast *whistles* from a garden-croft;
And gathering swallows *twitter* in the skies.

(John Keats: 'To Autumn')

PERSONIFICATION to give human qualities to inanimate or non-human things:

The hour-glass whispers to the lion's roar.

(W.H.Auden: 'Our Bias')

QUATRAIN a four-line unit of poetry, the most common length for a stanza.

RHYME the quality that distinguishes poetry from ordinary speech, though it is not necessarily present (as in blank verse — see above). It gives emphasis to meaning and unity to structure. Most often it is found at the ends of lines, though some poets use it within lines as well.

RHYTHM (see METRE)

SATIRE poetry, usually comic or witty, which yet has the serious purpose of reforming some aspect of society or human behaviour, e.g. Alexander Pope's *The Dunciad*.

SIMILE similar to the metaphor (see above), but usually introduced by 'like' or 'as':

71

Come with soft rounded cheeks and eyes *as bright*
As sunlight on a stream.   (Christina Rossetti: 'Echo')

SONNET   a poem of fourteen lines, divided into eight lines (octave) and six lines (sestet), usually concluding with a rhyming couplet. Shakespeare is the author of a famous sequence of sonnets.

SYMBOL   not merely a comparison (like a simile) or extended identification (like a metaphor) or even a more sustained analogy (like an image), a symbol represents a larger, more profound and complex idea than itself. In W.B. Yeats' poems, for example, the swan is symbolic of the poet's soul.

TONE   the result of the evolution of the subject of a poem by the poet. A frivolous tone suggests that the poet regarded the theme lightheartedly, as in 'The White Knight's Song' by Lewis Carroll. Then the tone might be melancholy, as in Christina Rossetti's 'Amor Mundi', or satirical (in T.S.Eliot's 'Whispers of Immortality') or anguished (in G.M. Hopkins' 'Thou Art Indeed Just, Lord') or exultant (in John Milton's 'On the Morning of Christ's Nativity'), and so on. The tone of a poem, the combination of subject and style, is the best guide to its meaning.